I0794904

THE EVANGELIST

These poems immerse the reader in the narrator's reckonings with what was given, and what was taken, by his father—a man who borrows his son's money for beer, challenges him to fist fights, tends a garden that yields more than they can eat, and mends broken things as best he can. In language that captures the rhythms of everyday speech, and line breaks that evoke both the dissonances and harmonies of memory, David Armand reveals the difficult beauty in a cigarette flicked in anger, a "wilting tree doused with lights," and "stars like buckshot across the sky," images that flicker with promise and sorrow. This book is suffused with gratitude, understanding, empathy, and loss—a celebration of the "pain exchanged and passed along...when someone says 'I love you.'"

—Robert Lee Kendrick, author of *What Once Burst with Brilliance* and *Winter Skin*

Good poems bring us home with them for a spell. They build trust over time and share their experiences with us bit by bit. Great poems, though, feel like home from their first line on. David Armand offers the reader great poems. They are about fathers, and sons, and of a world so real you can smell piney woods and see steam rising off a newborn foal. The joys, and pains, of these poems are at once familial and universal, individual and metonymic. There's not much more you could ask a poem to do, not much more a poet could deliver, than what Armand gives us here.

—Jack B. Bedell, author of *Color All Maps New* and Poet Laureate of Louisiana, 2017–2019

This is a beautiful collection. In poem after poem, David Armand recognizes the importance of the familial, the personal, and the ways in which memory lingers and creates new realities. The clarity of these poems—their unimpeded voice—reveals Armand's greatest strength: to tell stories and to tell them well. As in his fine novels, these poems resonate with aural lushness, but the sound never overwhelms the senses. Indeed, one gets the impression that a friend is present, recounting memories—a masterful raconteur whose poetic voice emanates with authenticity and even kindness. Armand's giftedness spans across genres: he is an excellent poet, one whose voice will sustain.

—William Wright, series editor of *The Southern Poetry Anthology* and author of *Grass Chapels*

Also by David Armand

NOVELS
The Pugilist's Wife
Harlow
The Gorge
The Lord's Acre

MEMOIR
My Mother's House

POETRY
The Deep Woods
Debt

THE EVANGELIST

[Poems]

David Armand

MERCER UNIVERSITY PRESS
Macon, Georgia
2022

MUP/ P649

Published by Mercer University Press
1501 Mercer University Drive
Macon, Georgia 31207

26 25 24 23 22 5 4 3 2 1

Books published by Mercer University Press are printed on acid-free paper that meets the requirements of the American National Standard for Information Sciences—Permanence of Paper for Printed Library Materials.

Printed and bound in the United States.

This book is set in ADOBE CASLON PRO.

Cover/jacket design by Burt&Burt.

ISBN 978-0-88146-855-7
Cataloging-in-Publication Data is available from the Library of Congress

Contents

IV.

V.

VI.

Acknowledgments

Grateful acknowledgment is made to the editors of the following journals in which some of these poems originally appeared, sometimes in slightly different form.

Arkansas Review: "The King on Beale Street"
Calliope: "Refraction"
The Cape Rock: "*Clair de Lune*" and "A Deer's Death"
Delta Poetry Review: "Blume with Chicken," "The Evangelist, " "Man with Mouthless Fish," "The Pink Pony Cafe," and "Stoop"
Eunoia Review: "After Quail Hunting," "Blood River, Springfield, Louisiana," "Early Morning in the Marsh," and "Fires"
Flash Fiction Press: "Wallet"
Foxglove Journal: "Cologne"
Furtive Dalliance: "Bail," "Coach," "Garden," "Go-Kart," and "Roadside Attractions"
Muddy River Poetry Review: "Truck"
The Penmen Review: "Anger" and "Rabbit Cage"
Poetry South: "Debt"
San Pedro River Review: "The Hitchhiker," "Horses at Night on a Highway in Virginia," "Mend," and "Night Terror"
The Texas Review: "The Deep Woods"
Town Creek Poetry: "Bridge," "Cello," "Hurt," "The Impressionist," and "Knife"
Twelve Mile Review: "At a Filling Station in Sledge, Mississippi" and "Bus"
"Photograph of My Father" was selected by WRBH Reading Radio in New Orleans as one of the winners of their inaugural poetry competition in 2015. The author is grateful to the staff at the radio station, particularly David Benedetto, for letting him and his family tour the studio.

And a very special debt of gratitude is owed to Jeff and Tobi Alfier at Blue Horse Press, who published two chapbooks, *The Deep Woods* (2015) and *Debt* (2018), in which some of these poems also appeared.

I.

Mare Foaling in Winter

Despite the cold the stall inside is warm.
It smells of dusty hay and lime,
the only light a single sixty watt bulb
hanging from an orange extension cord
which is stapled to a splintered rafter
and twists across the soffits like a snake.
The light fills the stall while outside
gray dawn comes cold and full
with winter's threat of sleet or even snow.

Inside the stall there's a father, a mother
and their three young children
surrounding a foaling brown mare.
They watch as she exhales warm breath
visible as smoke this winter morning
chuffing out from her large nostrils,
her eyes worried and far-away discs
as her dusty withers twitch and pulse,
sending a lethargic black fly alight.

The gnawed and serried boards around her
creak against the mare's sweat-streaked sides—
the giant hoops of her ribs and the life
inside of them pushing against the wall
as her whickering picks up and raises
the already-expectant pulse of everyone here.

They are all waiting.

The gray mud beneath them is soft
and cratered with the hoof prints
from the mare's carefully-shod hooves

and her many hours of pacing and stomping,
her halter clanging against her trough
as she scooped sweet feed into her mouth:
this same thing every day, but now she's giving
birth.

The family huddles and watches
as first the tiny forelegs and head come forth
slick and white and alive but stuck.
Then the foal stops moving.
The mare's sides contract.
And now nothing—a quiet tableau.
And all inside the stall stands still.
Then the man stands up and grabs
a pair of metal calf-pullers which he soaked
earlier this morning in a tub of soapy water.
He uses them now to bring the foal into existence,
pulling as gently as he would a child
as though he had done this a hundred times.

The young family watches as the foal emerges.
It shakes its little head and breaks the sac
which had held it for some three hundred days.
It tries already to stand on its spindling legs,
nudging toward its exhausted mother for milk.

The man puts down the calf-pullers now,
setting them on the ground in a bed of hay
and beside the rest of his tack and tools.
Then he goes over to sit with his family
to watch this new life nursing, breathing,
waking to the promise of what's to follow.

Hurt

My son was riding his bike
in the street yesterday
when he turned too sharp
fell down
and knocked out two of his teeth
against the cracked asphalt.

The blood was something to behold
coming out through his fingers
like that
as he ran toward me, crying,
stumbling across the yard
in his damp and muddy socks.

We put him in the car and drove
to the Emergency Room
but after almost three hours
without seeing a doctor
we left.
            It was getting too late.

My son was feeling better by then
though his lip was swollen
and his chin and hands were scraped up
as though someone had taken
a stub of sandpaper to them.

His white school shirt
had turned pink at the collar
where the blood and spit
had leaked from the throbbing sockets
in his gums

where his beautiful white teeth had been
but now were gone
lying somewhere by the ditch
beside our driveway.

That night as I tried to sleep
I fell into a dream
in which I was building a house.
It reached up to the sky
like a cathedral, that house,
but when I stepped back
to see the work I'd done
it all started to come down
raining split soffits and bricks,
all the dust and splinters now a thick cloud
bubbling up on the ground
around my feet.

My kids were there
and we were running now:
my daughter in my arms
crying something about her shoes—
that everything we had was gone.

And then I woke up.

I looked over at my two beautiful children
who were sleeping quietly
and I pulled the blanket over their legs,
tried to fall back asleep myself.
But it was useless.
So I got out of bed.

It was still dark while I made the coffee
then sat on the sofa and pet the dog,

watching the news on mute
so I wouldn't wake anyone up.

Rain all day, it showed,
the splotches on the radar
green and yellow and even red
in spots, moving across Louisiana
like someone dragging a sheet
over a field for a picnic.

This was fine by me:
I was taking off work anyway.
I needed to be home for a while.

Knife

My dad kept a shoebox full of knives
in his closet next to several boxes
of shotgun shells and his .38 revolver—
it was all on a top shelf
and out of our reach.

Sometimes he would take it down
for us to look at
since some of the knives in that box were mine
or otherwise my brother's.

We each had a Swiss Army knife in there
which held a small blade,
tweezers, a nail file, scissors,
and a little plastic toothpick
you could pull out of that glossy red handle
with your fingernail.

Then there were two folding knives
with varnished beechwood handles
where our initials
had been engraved with a woodburning tool,
its orange metal tip smoldering
until there was a dark brown *D.A.* on mine
and a *B.A.* on my brother's.

But my favorite knife was one
I got at the parish fair one night
as we were walking down
the dusty, haystrewn midway.
My dad was in front of us,
his faded brown boots

stepping over myriad rills
of spilled drinks,
cigarette butts, and Coke cups,
over endless yards
of orange and black extension cords
through which all the power flowed,
lighting up the drooping strands of bulbs overhead
and the yellow and red ones on the Ferris wheel
and the many blinking lights
on the Gravitron, the Scrambler, the bumper cars—
all encircled by metal barricades
and lines of people waiting in the balding grass
to get on, the tips of their cigarettes glowing
like lightning bugs.

                    As we walked by
there were grizzled men in booths
calling out to us from behind a scrim
of neon-lit cigarette smoke,
the smell of funnel cakes
                              cotton candy
                                        popcorn
                                                  livestock
telling everyone to take a chance:
one dollar one try
three dollars five tries.

You could win it all, they said.
Stuffed animals, posters,
a balsawood plane you launched
with a rubber band.

But my dad ignored them,
pitching his own cigarette
into the dust.

We kept walking,

stopping only when we saw some knives
hanging from a sheet of pocked corkboard
in one of the painted wooden booths.
These were Bowie knives, he told us,
and he wanted my brother and me
each to have one.

                    It was important, he said,
that we had some good knives
in our collection
and that we knew how to use them,
to revere them for their power
and what they could do to you
if you weren't careful
(he had been stabbed when he was a kid
playing around with a switchblade—
the one with the pearl handle
that he still kept in the shoebox
in his closet next to ours).

Then he bought us each one of the knives
from that carnival barker,
handing us the little box they came in,
and he let us keep them clipped
to our belts for the rest of the night,
though later they would end up in that shoe-
box with the others, only to be seen
every once in a while.

And, Lord, I can still remember
that knife's black leather sheath,
how it was cracked and faded
around the edges,

how it snapped shut
over the brass crosspiece
to keep the blade from slipping out.

I remember the way the wood handle
felt in my hand—the heft of it—
how the blade sounded when you slid
it out the sheath
                    and when you put it back in.

Wallet

Christmas morning and you've already opened up all your gifts:
the accumulation of a meager year, but still you're glad
for this airtight ammunition box made of industrial plastic,
even though you have no shotgun shells to put in it yet
and your .410's locked away in your father's closet.

You're looking at this camouflage-green box and imagining
it filled with rows of ammunition, and then chambering
one of those red plastic shells in your gun's dark barrel
in hopes of killing a duck or a squirrel or a rabbit.

This is when your father comes into your room.
He looks down at you looking down at that box
and he asks you how much money you got for Christmas
that year. You tell him (it's really not that much
since you're only nine and your family's poor anyway)
and then he asks if he can borrow it.

Although he doesn't say, you already know
what it's for, but you tell him "yes" anyway.
What else are you supposed to say?
He promises he'll pay you back. With interest.
As if that makes handing over your Christmas money
so that your dad can buy beer with it a better deal.

You open your Velcro wallet—the sound like tearing
a sheet of construction paper in a quiet classroom—
and you pull out the crumpled ones and fives.
He takes them without ever looking directly at you.
"Thanks, babe," he says. "I'll pay you back. Don't worry."

Then he leaves your room, head down, headed
to whatever dark place would be open on Christmas
and serving alcohol to men without families
and indiscriminately to those who left theirs at home
beside a wilting Christmas tree doused with lights.

The Impressionist

The low-green light from the console
stretching over your face, hands, body,
windows cracked to let the smoke out—
some cheap pot's all it takes to turn
my head into a landscape of memories
like I'm blurred across a canvas
of one of those French painters—
Impressionists, I think they're called.

I slept through most of Art History,
but I remember two or three slides
clicking through the projector's wheel
like gears locking home in a new transmission—
a sound I dream about, would pay to hear
even if I didn't give a damn about cars,
couldn't rebuild an engine in forty hours flat
or trace a leak in a fuel line.

Those foggy landscapes, smeared-on skies,
smiling waitresses in a fuzzy café,
stuff I never really understood, much less
cared about. But right now, with the radio
hovering over our voices, and the engine's hum
almost visible through the windshield,
your arms are soft and illuminated like candles,
keeping my eyes open, waiting for that next click.

The Map

I didn't know exactly where I was,
but the town of Waveland, Mississippi, is small
so I wasn't too worried when I rode over some train tracks
and wound up on a sandy asphalt road
that stretched along the Gulf Coast
like a plumb line laid flat all the way to Bay St. Louis.

I turned around, stopped at a convenience store
whose gas pumps had yellow tape around them
that said OUT OF SERVICE, but the store itself
was still open—a sign for ICE, BEER, MILK, BREAD
lit up behind the smudged glass and flickering
or faded in the places where the neon had burned out.

I went inside and picked up a map from off the counter,
paid for it, then brought it back out to my car,
unfolding the giant page against the steering wheel.
I looked for where I was among the sprawling lines
(right next to the train tracks at this gas station here)
and then I traced with my finger to where I was trying to go:

Coral Street was on the other side of Highway 90, it said,
just down Waveland Avenue and then off Avenue B,
buried among a patch of woods and manmade canals.
I folded the map into a more manageable size,
put it on the empty passenger seat so I could still see
the roads I'd need to take to get from here to there.

It took me about ten minutes to get to that gravel road.
It was walled in on either side by pines, their boles grayed
by the dust chuffing out from underneath my car's slowing tires,
crunching the rocks like tumbrel wheels

carrying me on some dark but necessary journey.

And then I stopped.
                                        The map still sat on the seat,
one of its corners furling in on itself
as I looked out the window to my right,
where just behind a chest-high fence—
whose boards were warped and where poison ivy
grew through its slats like wires in an unfinished house—
a small camper sat. Its windows were boarded up
with sheets of moldy, chalk-marked plywood,
and a rusted-out truck was parked beside it.
There was a naked lightbulb just above the front door.
It was on. Someone was inside, in the dark, encapsulated
by the smell of mold and God-knows-what else,
just waiting there for the day that I would show up
like this. But I couldn't get out of the car.
All I could do was sit there, the engine starting
to get overheated, the gauge moving slowly to *H*
like a finger wiping off a mistake on a chalkboard.

I was fifteen years old, couldn't fold a map,
couldn't even buy a pack of cigarettes
without a fake ID, and yet here I was
sitting in my car in front of the dilapidated trailer
where my mother lived.
                                        My mother.
Whom I hadn't seen in a dozen years
and wouldn't see for a dozen more,
when I would be a father myself
and would remember that run-down camper
as I left it in a cloud of gray and lonely dust.

Clair de Lune

This is a memory I don't have:
sitting side by side on a rickety piano bench,
my legs too short to reach the floor
        (since I'm just a boy)
as you play *Clair de Lune* for me,
your fingers carefully pressing out each note:
the sharps, the flats, those soft impressionistic chords.
When you're done, you bend to kiss
me on the head. You tell me that you love me.
I'm the only son you would ever have.

How I do remember you, though, is like this:
finding you on the floor of your trailer,
the bottle of Librium beside you open,
half of them gone, the rest strewn
across the linoleum like black-and-baby-blue gravel
culled from the bottom of a dirty fish tank,
your shallow, staccato breath
barely coming through your half-opened mouth
as though filled with wads of cotton,
unable to say a word.

Mend

The first time I met my mother,
        when I was twenty,
we stayed up the whole night talking
        and playing the piano.

She could still play *Clair de Lune*
        from memory
and I remember her hands on the keys,
        how she'd placed her palms on my face
when she first saw me, taking in the sight
        of her only child.
She said she hadn't even seen a picture of me
        since she had given me up for adoption.

And now it was like trying to fit
        all those years
into just a few short hours
        —the talking and the music.
What can you possibly say to someone
        so that they'll know who you are?

When it was finally time for me to go,
        my mother fell down
onto the kitchen floor, her eyes rolling
        back to their jaundiced whites,
her legs and arms flailing then seizing
        on the cold beige tiles.

        She later said it was so I wouldn't leave;
but still I rode in the back of an ambulance
        with her, held her hand and stayed up
all night in the ER until she finally walked out

on her own. She was just fine.
I slept the whole next day.

Before she disappeared again
for what would be another dozen years,
my mother stitched a button back onto my shirt.
It's something simple, I know,
but I still remember that—we were in the kitchen
again, the same one where she had fallen down—
and the button had just come off,
like things sometimes do.

So she said she wanted to fix it for me.
And even though I didn't know
that would be the last time I'd see her
for a good while—finding her years later
on the floor of her trailer next to an empty bottle
of pills and a yellowed program
from a piano recital she had given when she was a teenager—
I handed her my shirt.

Then I watched as she threaded a needle
with her quivering fingers,
becoming the mother I think she wanted
to be—and could have been—
if only the world hadn't been so hard on her.

For now, though, the button was slowly mended
back into its place.
Where it belonged.

Cello

The moment before the strings suddenly snapped
free from his instrument's smoothed surface,
sending the sound of a shotgun blast
out from the pulpit and over the pews
outside, down the pigeon-cowled stairway
of the St. Louis Cathedral at morning mass,
the boy behind the cello had his eyes closed
and was thinking of the time he got lost
in a cane field as a child,

                                        walking down
the rows and rows and kicking at the stalks,
his three feet two inches a third the size
of the swaying stems: a maze of yellow-brown
surrounding him on every side but up

where the sky was blue, clear blue, and cold,
but as the boy looked there and saw it getting dark
he ran the way he thought he knew was home
until it all began to look the same—
the stalks like living light poles on each side,
confusing him, like the things around us do
when we're young and scared and can hardly tell
the ground from rows of cane or evening sky—
and he started to call for his father, who broke
his way through the stalks until he was there,

scooping his son up in his farm-hardened arms
and then holding him snug against his warm work shirt
telling him, "I'm here, stop crying, I'm here"
as if this was all that needed to be said

so that when the boy opened his eyes, he was back
in the cathedral and could see his father now
sitting in the pews with everybody else
not owing a thought to anything but faith—
faith his son would be okay, that this, like time
would pass and the noise of those broken strings
would fade away into the sanctuary
while the orchestra picked up where it left off

and the boy put down his bow and just listened then
as if nothing bad had ever happened to him.

II.

Roadside Attractions

Driving down Highway 190 on my way to work,
I noticed a news truck from one of the local stations
parked on the narrow gravel shoulder of the road.

It was next to a concrete guardrail
which fronted a small creek, its brown stagnant water
curtained on all sides by bright green kudzu
and thin wispy trees.

Next to the creek,
I saw a cameraman, the silver-and-black metal
of his equipment winking in the sunlight
as he trained his lens on a female reporter,
a raincoat on and mud boots past her knees.

The water behind her was the color of tea
whose surface was mapped with algae,
otherwise still in this windless evening.

Then, as if by some strange design, my truck radio
started telling the story of why I'd seen
what I'd just seen: the night before, it said,
a woman had driven her SUV over that guardrail.

A trucker spotted it the next morning,
pulled over, waded through the weeds
and the thigh-deep mud. But nothing stirred.

Later that night, when I was driving back home,
I saw a deer coming up from out the ditch—
not far from where the accident had happened.
The deer was about to cross. One more second
and it would've been in my path.

Instead, my brights just grazed his eye
as I watched him disappear
back into those dark woods,
where so much, it seems, goes to either live or die.

At a Filling Station in Sledge, Mississippi

This is the kind of town where folks say
don't blink or you'll miss it, so you slow down
and pull in because the sign outside says GAS
and because it's the only place you've seen
open for miles:
                    even though two fat hens roost
on top of a rusty oil drum, then slowly feather
themselves onto the dry, clay-reddened gravel
as you drive up and the rocks pop under your tires.

The hens peck at the dust and make their way
toward a man who's half-sleeping, hunched
over in a green plastic lawnchair,
the stretched slats creaking as he startles up
at the sound of your car when you stop,
get out, shut the door. And now the engine ticks
as it cools under the sun-tired hood.

                                        "Can I *help* you?"
he says, as though there might be something more
than gas that you need.

                                        You take a second
before you answer him, consider what you'd ask
if you were him and he were you instead,
if you weren't just passing through, but called—
like he must do—this lonely place your home.

Would there be more hope in your question too, a need
for someone to want more than you can sell them:
a conversation maybe, a handshake, anything to remind
you that the world knows you're here?

Bridge

We're driving across the Causeway,
twenty-four miles over black water,
and making our way to New Orleans
for a late-night Mardi Gras parade
when a car passes us on our left
and the passenger flicks a cigarette
out the window. It hits our windshield
and a slew of orange sparks spreads
over the glass like a puff of snow.

From the back seat, we hear our dad
cursing and then see the orange tip
of the push-button lighter as he lights
his own cigarette and starts puffing
on it wildly. He's speeding up the car,
trying to catch the one that just passed,
our mom pulling on his arm for him
to slow down before he gets us killed.

When he finally catches up to them,
he rolls down the window, the rush
of air coming in cold and with rain,
and then he flicks his own cigarette
out at the car that just passed us.

Revenge. The driver and passenger
look confused as the orange sparks
bloom over their hood now, and die.
Then we slow back down, headlights
from the cars behind us growing larger
and larger in our sideview mirrors
as the lake on either side spreads out
flat as a fallow field in autumn.

Night Terror

I hate bridges, and in my dreams
I'm always going over one,
a black narrow line stretching
up into the vast, cloud-filled sky
like God's dark finger reaching down
and touching the road in front of the car.

I try to turn around but can't,
my ears popping now with the altitude,
and when I finally reach the summit
I can see over the metal guardrail
the angry, roiling water beating
against the pylons, which are always
twined with metal stairs, leading
up (or down) like strands of DNA.

People are usually going over these steps,
moving slowly and with blank faces,
most of them falling somehow
only to be sliced in two by the myriad cables
that are holding up the bridge.

Then *I* go over—either in my car
or after having jumped—
all the air in my lungs sucked out
as I wake up finally,
screaming and gasping for breath.

The Hitchhiker

My father was coming home.
It was three in the morning,
and he was driving down Hwy 47
in Chalmette, Louisiana.
This was after twelve long hours
of trawling for shrimp
in Lake Borgne and the bayous
surrounding it—returning
with his nets empty.

Then, in that early morning dark,
he saw a hunched-over old man
hitchhiking on the side of the road.
My father slowed, then stopped.
Decided to pick him up.
After all, the man looked harmless,
not to mention it was cold.

The cracked domelight glowed
as the hitchhiker got in the cab,
and my father saw his dirty clothes,
long beard—the smell of him—
and thought he was doing
a good thing: until he pulled
off and the old man grabbed
a knife from his coat.

He held its rusty blade against
my father's throat, told him
to give over his wallet.
So my father leaned forward,
not saying a word, one hand

still on the steering wheel—
and reaching with the other
as if carefully going for
what the old man wanted.

But he grabbed a gun instead,
pushing its cold barrel
against the old man's head, knocking
away the knife, slamming the brakes
and forcing the hitchhiker out
before his truck even came to a stop.

And I still imagine that old man
on the cold gravel shoulder,
watching the red taillights
from my father's truck
diminish now into a single point,
astonished at his turn of bad luck
and wondering who in the hell
had just picked him up.

A Deer's Death

A trail of upturned mud left in the grass
and several small trees that had been cracked
in half or smashed along the narrow path,
and pulled-down power lines like rubber bands
were all I had to understand the sight
I saw through my windshield, blurred and foggy
as it was with the rain that still poured down,
but it was certainly enough for me
to figure out what nature must've done
to bring so many people out of bed
like witnesses to some great tragedy
or the unlikely bearers of a weight
that rested in ballooning, rain-drenched flesh
discarded in the grass when those swift winds
came snake-like from the clouds, and rumbling,
swept up the little doe from her wandering
over the dewy leaves and grass she ate
and spun her left and right 'til life left her,
spitting her out like something that went stale,
all the stuff that made it good now gone.

Dead Fox

Early in the morning and it's still dark
as I drive down Highway 22 to work.
The road cuts through marsh and woods
with a scrim of fog hanging low against
the asphalt.
                    It comes up unexpectedly,
a lump in this throat of narrow highway,
so that at first I hardly register the tuft
of orange fur clumped with white and black.
A fox.
          Out from the woods and over this strip
of highway, only to be hit by some car or truck.
The last thing it ever saw were the headlights
bearing down on it like two bright tunnels
of light, spackled with black floating dust motes
and whatever other debris we find on the road
when we're driving to work after a long night.

Horses at Night on a Highway in Virginia

—for my father

It's a late drive through the Shenandoah Valley,
the road cascading down in mineral-stippled clay,
old miners' houses pocking the hills and deep swales
like outposts on another planet.

The headlights graze
all of this as the truck eases around the bends,
occasionally edging itself off onto the shoulder
where the gravel pops, the cracked asphalt hissing
under the tires.
But the driver's tired,
doesn't hear the hoof-
beats or see the chuffs of cloudy breath as a band of horses
pummels a nearby field on their way to a bigger pasture,
just on the other side of this lonely, dark, and quiet road:
where there is no fence like the one they've just broken
through as their owner sleeps inside next to his wife,
tendrils of smoke whispering out of their tin chimney
above the leaning clapboard house that would otherwise
never be a part of this memory—if it weren't for these horses.

But here they come! There's no time to stop as they cross
the driver's path: one of them hit outright, a headlight smashing
against its shoulder, its legs breaking instantly as its body falls
and goes under the tires. A few seconds later it is painted red
by the taillights as the truck comes to a stop and waits, the engine
ticking.

The horse is still breathing, spurts of dusty air vibrating
through its bloodied nostrils, its eye black and glassy, wet-rimmed

as it stares up into the night. That deep spackling of stars
        overhead.
The other horses have come back to look; they circle the truck
and brush their long heads against the cracked windshield
as the other one lay dying on the road.
                                                            Their hooves clack
on the pavement, a metronome in the night: In these mountains,
these dark hills where all living things must eventually succumb.

III.

Debt

A knock on the front door as you play in the den
with your brother and your older sister.
Your mom gets up from the sofa to answer it
and you hear her screaming as some man pushes
his way into the house, a gun pointing
at her head. She tells you and your siblings
to run, hide under the bed.

And you can't remember
anything else from that morning except for this:
the man asking where your father was, saying
he's there to collect some money, a payment
on a payday loan. But your father's at work
and probably wouldn't pay this man anyway,
even if he was here and could see his kids
hiding in a quivering row underneath their bed.
Like the three little pigs in that story your mom reads,
the one about the big bad wolf who blows down
all their poorly-made houses—all except for one.

Power

The boy's father never kept a bank account
so each month on payday he'd cash
his checks at the grocery store
for a fee.

            Then the boy would watch
him as he counted out stacks
of tens, twenties, and hundreds
on the wobbly kitchen table,
putting it all on top of the refrigerator
in a fat envelope,

                        which got smaller
and smaller as the month wore on:
all those wrinkled bills disappearing
like air slowly leaking from an old tire
or water dripping from a rusty faucet—
things that would be better off fixed
if only there was enough to pay for it all.

But there never was.

                                    So that one day,
when a man in dark blue overalls
came to cut their power off,
the boy watched his mother beg:
I have kids, she'd said.
How are they gonna do their homework?
She was crying.

                        The man ignored her,
but the boy could've sworn

from where he was watching
out his bedroom window
that the man looked ashamed
of the job he had come to do,
seemed embarrassed to be there
as he flipped the switch and sent
them all into darkness.

Coach

The first day of class he made fun of me
for my long hair so I didn't like him much.
A few weeks in and nothing had changed
until one day he started talking about his child-
hood, how his father bought whiskey instead
of paying the bill to heat their house, how he
had only one pair of brown Dickies to wear
to school for the entire year and if they got holes
in them, then tough luck.
                                        He told us about the times
his father hit him, and how finally he had moved out
and signed up for the army. Vietnam. His buddies
over there dying in his lap like damp sacks of rice.
How he finally ended up here, teaching kids like me
with long hair and grease under their fingernails,
I guess I'll never know.

Economics

Sometimes my father rolled his own cigarettes
with cheap tobacco he bought by the pound
from Walgreens.
                              It came in big yellow bags,
like dog food, but with a flimsy plastic window
in front so that you could see what was inside.

It was cheap, that tobacco, but it yielded
more cigarettes for your money,
and that's all that mattered to my father,
a man who grew up and died poor.

The last time I saw him I was nineteen
and had been an on-again-off-again smoker myself,
ever since I was twelve and stole a pack of Carltons
from my grandmother, who bought them by the carton.

I smoked my first one in the woods behind our trailer
and then kept the rest of the pack in a Cracker Jack tin
under a rotten log. I would smoke one every day
after school until the pack was gone; then I buried
the empty box in the dirt.

                                        When I was eighteen,
I started smoking Camels or sometimes Marlboros
since you could get two packs for the price of one
from a place called River Forest Mart in Covington,
and because Mickey Rourke and Sean Penn smoked
those and I thought they looked cool doing it.

Eventually I gave it up, though.

But not before a meeting
I had for work one night, which ended
at one of my colleagues' houses,
and where she offered me a cigarette
from a stash she kept in her freezer.

I smoked it, flicking the ashes
into a black plastic ashtray, then blowing
out that last cold drag of smoke—
one I would never have to pay for again.

Shotgun

It was a Remington .410 Wingmaster
I'd owned since I was a boy.
I had learned to shoot with it.
First at beer cans and then at paper targets
nailed to a pine tree in our back yard.
Then finally using it to kill
more quail and squirrels and ducks
than you could shake a stick at,
as my father would've said.

My father. The man who walked
into a pawnshop one day
with me following closely behind him
as he went up to the counter
and hocked every gun he had,
just so that we could eat that month.

What does that sort of memory teach a boy,
if not to do the same thing himself one day?
Twenty years later when his own family's hungry—
leaving them out in the car as he goes inside
to pawn the only gun he has left,
which he had used once to bring down a squirrel
as it scampered up the side of an oak tree
before it was filled with a bunch of tiny pellets.

Bail

The first time my father was arrested
we put up our property for his bond.
After that when we couldn't keep him
out of jail—DWIs, resisting arrest,
driving under a suspended license,
illegal possession of a firearm,
intimidation, disorderly conduct, assault—
we had to let him stay there
until he saw a judge. The final verdict
was five years. My dad had done time
before, so I was surprised to find him
sitting at the kitchen table the night before
we dropped him off to start his sentence,
smoking and sobbing quietly. He flicked
his ashes into a coffee cup that was stained
brown from years of use, but also neglect.

Arrest

My father hated being told what to do,
started smoking Marlboro reds
when he was only nine years old, wouldn't even quit
after his dad grounded him for six months straight—
just cracked the window in his room and blew
the smoke out, flicked his ashes in the yard.

                                        Then he got older.
And the things he was expected to do, but didn't,
piled up on him like unwashed clothes on the floor.
His life just got harder and harder.

He was in jail a lot, had to adhere to another code there,
a whole different ethic; this seemed to suit him though.
Their laws were based on honor and respect, he would tell us,
something he said our society just didn't value anymore.

The other inmates liked him, called him chief;
they all knew that he was in for his third DWI,
driving without a license, carrying a sawed-off shotgun
under his seat. Resisting arrest: he had kicked
out the window of a cop car
after they'd cuffed him, then held his head
against their cruiser's scalding hood
until his face blistered.
Finally shoved him in:

                                a slab of meat in an oven
that when left for too long just burns.

Anger

Every weekend my father sat
on the sofa all day watching
movies like *Lethal Weapon*,
Platoon, *Lonesome Dove*,
Tombstone, and all five *Rocky*s
back to back.

His favorite one
was *The Abyss* with Ed Harris
and Mary Elizabeth Mastrantonio
and sometimes he'd watch it—
rewind the tape he'd rented
from John's Curb Market,
which was down the road in Folsom
and where he also bought
cigarettes, beer, and once or twice
a Slush Puppy for my brother and me—
and then he'd watch it again.

You could hear the old VCR
humming and clicking
all the way from our room
at the other end of the trailer
as my father rewound the tape
and watched that movie about
underwater oil rig workers
who encounter an alien species
as they try to help disarm
a nuclear warhead on a submarine—
all while a vicious hurricane spins
above the surface of the ocean.

He'd drink can after can of Bud
and smoke Marlboro reds,
flecking the old coffee table—
which was made out of a hatch
door from a boat he'd once owned—
with gray ashes.

                    Times when the batteries
in the remote controller stopped working,
he'd yell for my brother or me to come
into the den to change the channel for him
or turn up the sound, fast forward the previews
for the upcoming features he didn't care about.
"Oh, *boys*," he'd yell. "Get your asses in here."
We always thought we were in trouble at first,
but then we'd get to the den and he'd just tell
us what to do. It was embarrassing for everyone.

Other times when we had to walk past him
to get in the kitchen for something to eat,
we always ducked beneath the TV screen
so we wouldn't get in his way, but even still
he'd pop up from his spot on the sofa,
unpredictably and without warning sometimes,
and he'd yell, "What the *hell* are you looking
at, son? You want to *fight*? *Huh*? You think
you can whip my ass?"

                              "No," we'd say back,
softly, like stepping over a rat trap, or holding
a loaded shotgun, keeping it pointed at the sky
so it wouldn't accidentally go off.

Mischief

An image: two metal garbage cans on either side of the street.
They're tied together by their squeaky handles with jute twine
found in someone's father's garage next to a bottle
of half-empty Miller Lite.

The string is old, which is good
because it droops loose enough so the tired drivers
heading home won't see it, won't know what the hell
just happened when the cans slam against their cars
as that string pulls taut and metal collides with metal,
a loud scraping noise.
Something unnatural but thrilling
to the group of fifteen-year-old boys
hiding behind the bushes off to the side, the orange glow
of their stolen cigarettes lighting up their faces
and eyes as the brake lights come on
and the driver gets out from behind the wheel,
cursing as those kids just try to hold in their laughter.
Not an easy thing to do having fun like this.
And when the car pulls off they'll do it all over again.

You should know that one of these boys is my father.
He's the youngest of the group. Only nine and already smoking,
hanging out with these hoodlums, as his mother calls them.

And this too: that tomorrow they'll throw water balloons
into people's houses, watching the living room carpet soak
up the spill, and then running down the sidewalk
before Mrs. Ordes can see their faces well enough to tell

their fathers. Those men who come home from work tired
and pissed off, just looking for a good reason to whale

on their sons, slipping a cracked leather belt
from their greasy work pants and watching the welt
it makes on the backs of their boys' legs, something
almost delicate about those pink blooms of flesh.
How they blister and burn.

That's probably what they're worrying over as one of them finally
tosses in the balloon, not filled with water like they thought
(the kid who did it *said* they'd be surprised)
but a pint of white paint which spreads out over the carpet
like blood, thick and slow to move. The horror stamped
on all their faces, a silent tableau. And then the realization:
This woman standing before them knows all of their fathers,
will surely tell who did it. And they'll all have hell to pay,
a hell these boys will pass on to their own sons one day—
like Adam's curse, their pain exchanged and passed along
for when their sons do something dumb, which they'll inevitably do,
until someone stops them, says, "Come here, son. I love you."

IV.

Mirror

When I was a kid we used to go this place
called The Pizza Man in Covington.
It was one of about three restaurants
where you could eat back then.

We went there all the time, my mom, dad,
brother, grandparents, then after, we all walked
around the corner to the Video Co-Op
and rented VHS tapes and Nintendo games.

It was a good time, my dad would drink beer
and the jukebox would play old songs
from the sixties and seventies. You could watch
the guy flipping pizza dough into saucers
through the finger-printed glass that looked
into the kitchen.

                    I still go there on my birthday
every year, even though my dad's dead,
so are my grandparents; and everyone else
has all gone their own way. Married, moved, etc.

The place hasn't changed at all in twenty years.
They still have the same paper menu, the same songs
on the jukebox, the same pictures on the wall:
pizza boxes with funny drawings on the covers,
framed puzzles of the Sistine Chapel, the Last Supper,
the same dim lighting and skein of flour on the floor.

But these days I go with my wife and my own two kids.
Just to remember good things about my life,
to share them with my family so they'll have something
nice to remember me by.

And it always socks me right in the gut,
the memory of it all, like a different life
I'm watching on TV or something.

But nothing like this: last night, we went there
and I took my son to the bathroom
after we had finished eating.
I was already full of nostalgia and longing,
so when I saw him looking in the mirror,
it occurred to me that I had probably looked
in that exact same mirror thirty years ago—
when I was the age he is now: his face becoming
my face, his hands my hands, time curving

in on itself, like the ends of a sheet of paper—
or those folding pictures from *Mad* magazine
like I used to tack onto my wall as a kid—
the ones that when you bend them in such a way,
what once seemed muddled now reveals
something entirely new and surprising.

Cologne

It was a mirrored, wooden cabinet
hung at about eye-level so he could see
himself before he left for work
in the morning, when it was still dark out
and everyone else was asleep and warm.

But he kept nothing but cologne in there,
bottles and bottles of it: Brut, Old Spice,
Pierre Cardin, English Leather, Coty Musk,
Stetson, Aqua Velva, Afta, Skin Bracer,
Preferred Stock, Aspen. Cheap stuff

his kids gave him, or maybe he bought it
himself at the drugstore for under ten bucks
so he'd have some variety in the morning,
some choice in how he presented himself
to a world where he didn't have many choices,

a world that was hard on him, and one he'd leave
far too soon: just after a meager Christmas one year
at only forty-two years old, all those cheap bottles
collecting dust now, their contents slowly evaporating
until the day comes when hardly anything is left in them.

Play

My father didn't play with us much when we were kids.
Our mom said he wasn't really the playful *type*, never was,
so we just had to take what we could get from him.

Which sometimes meant letting him lob softballs
at us from atop the trampoline, or holding us
under water in the pool for just a little bit too long.
I remember the panic just before breaking the skin
of the water's cool, chlorinated surface, then hearing
him laugh in that way which could only be funny
if you were on the right side of the joke: we never were.
He always let us go—eventually—but the promise
of danger and risk when it came to playing
with our father tugged at everything we did,
like an undertow, a threat more felt than seen.

This also meant letting our father win at things
so he wouldn't get mad, like that one time
we beat him at basketball and he punished us
on our knees, the granules of driveway concrete
pressing into our skin as we tried to figure out
what we had done wrong. Eventually we learned.
After that we always made sure to lose, fumbling
the ball around until he had a solid lead. He told
us we'd get better if we practiced, if we'd just stop
wasting so much time in our room. Playing Nintendo.
Or whatever it was he thought we did in there all day.

Rabbit Cage

My brother and I are playing outside
while our dad nails together the frame
for a rabbit cage. It's for our sister
who's out at the store with Mom.
They've taken the only car we have:
a blue Pinto we rent for sixty dollars
a week, a car so small my brother and I
have to ride in the hatchback trunk
when we take my sister to school
in the mornings. It's always cold
back there, even with the heater on.

We write our names on the glass.

Anyway, in the midst of the noise
of hammer against wood and nail,
we hear my father grunt in pain.
Then we hear him calling for help.

We run over to see he's nailed
his hand to the side of the cage.
How he did this I'll never know.
But he is losing a lot of blood,
his face is pale, his eyes are rolled
up to their white and bloodshot rims.

We help him get loose.

When our mom and sister get home,
they seem hard pressed to puzzle out
the rabbit cage leaning on its side,
but after a few minutes of explaining,

we all squeeze back into the blue Pinto
and drive to the hospital, sit there
for hours, then go back home, taking
turns in the one tiny bathroom,
washing ourselves and getting
ready for the next long day ahead,
as if all of this has happened before
and will continue to happen again
so long as we are poor and have
to do so much with so little.

Garden

It was around thirty feet long
by twelve feet wide, framed with railroad ties
that smelled like creosote as they baked
in the sun. They were stacked in threes,
the space inside filled with damp leaves,
eggshells, coffee grounds, and horse manure,
all covered with a layer of fresh topsoil.

I don't know why my dad built it, or even wanted to
in the first place. He didn't really like being outside
except to maybe sit on the porch and drink Budweisers
from a can. Smoke cigarettes.

But one year I remember him setting up a trellis
made out of chickenwire and some wooden stakes
which edged the garden and was eventually filled
with vines from tomato plants and squash.

He grew corn and cantaloupe, merlitons, red potatoes,
even planted a row of peach trees on the other side
of the yard, their branches laden with fruit
and drooping onto the grass so that we couldn't fill
our old wheelbarrow fast enough.

Most of them rotted.

                                        He had a fig tree too
which eventually grew higher than our roof,
its gigantic leaves covering the satellite dish.
We'd have to go outside and trim them back
just so that we could get a signal inside.

He grew all of these things so fast we could never eat it
and so he took the fruit to work in Walmart bags
and gave them to his coworkers.

My mom canned
some of the figs in little glass Mason jars and made
pepper jelly and fig preserves, which I would use
on peanut butter sandwiches when we ran
out of Smucker's.

Yet despite this overabundance
and the not-knowing-what-to-do
with all the things he grew,
my dad kept gardening anyway.
Kept at it for several years, furrowing
the rows of damp soil every new season.

It was like an addiction.

And I still remember how he worked every evening
in his jeans and flip-flops, a cool can of Bud cratered
in the grass next to him. And never too far out of reach.

Fires

1.

I was younger than my kids are now,
probably by at least a couple of years,
when I told my brother to stick a key
in the electrical socket in our room.
I sat behind him and pretended
we were driving down some highway
when he stuck in the key, and the sparks
shot out blue and white
with yellow traces of flame crawling
up the wainscoting, turning it black,
almost as dark as the room became
when the breaker finally tripped
and set the whole house to darkness.

The stars were buckshot across the sky
outside our square little window
which let in a cylinder of moonlight
while we sat there stunned and blank-faced
as mannequins, our reddening cheeks
waxing in the now-crackling firelight.

Before we could even move, me or him,
let alone call out for help,
our dad came in and pushed us both back
and, in what seemed the same motion, grabbed
one of our toy swords from off the floor
and knocked the key from the socket
until it lay black-edged on the carpet
like a scrap of steel discarded from its forge.

2.

Years later, when we were both teenagers,
my brother and I and two of our cousins
were pulling Black Cats from the single fuse
that held them together, then tossing
the orphaned fireworks into a metal lid
that we had pried from a tin of popcorn
which someone had given us that Christmas.
I'm not sure why, but one of our cousins lit
the Black Cat he was holding, then pitched
it into the lid with the unlit ones,
which all seemed to be waiting there
like a nest of angry black moccasins.

The little explosions, cumulatively, were loud,
the noise doubled by the echo from the metal lid.
And this time it was our mom, not our father,
running into the room to see what we had done.

The ceiling was already black. The gray smoke
was hanging around our shoulders and chests now
as it made its slow ascent up and then out of our room
through an open window and then into the yard.

3.

Now that I'm a father, I'm thinking about these things
after my kids brought a lit candle into their room today
and left it there—those same flames from my childhood
crawling up their wall as I ran into the house,
the smoke already thick and black,
chuffing up against the ceiling like a dark cumulus cloud,
as if it were being puffed out from a squeezed accordion,
the smoke alarm buzzing, my lungs hot and clenching.

I pushed things out of the way that were within the fire's reach—
a dresser, a nighttable, some stuffed animals, a few pillows.
I didn't know what else to do.

Then a man who had been doing some work in our yard
was in the room with me, not saying anything
as he sprayed a mist of sodium bicarbonate
from a chipped, red fire extinguisher he had in his truck,
suffocating the fire as though it had never been.
Now all that was left was the thick smoke,
and me still standing there in the dark—by myself
since that man had walked back out, still not saying anything.
I opened the window so I could let the rest of the smoke clear.

Bus

It was already dark when I drove up,
easing my truck over the broken asphalt,
a skein of gravel popping under the tires
as I found a far-off spot to park.

I was only fourteen, maybe fifteen, but here I was,
pulling in to work on a weeknight after school:
one of the first jobs I ever had, and my first shift there.

It was at an old pizza place called BJ's—
drowsing at the end of a half-empty strip mall,
past the old K & B drugstore with its purple sign,
the Delchamp's supermarket, a Payless Shoes
and a Hallmark store, all closed for the night.

I eased in under one of the dim floodlights
that pocked the lot and cast warm yellow circles
swarming with bugs and buzzing overhead,
illuminating the myriad veins of tar
that filled the cracked asphalt lot. I parked.

Then I put on the netted trucker's hat, the same dull red
as the itchy shirt they had given me when I was hired,
stuck my name tag on, and opened the door to get out.

When I got inside, the manager, Cindy, showed me
how to clock in, the yellowed punch card with a space
for me to write my name clicking under the metal press
as I slid it through, then stuck it in an empty slot on the wall.

"You wanna Coke or somethin?" she asked, smacking her gum.
I told her no thanks and then she showed me a stack of plastic bins
in the corner of the fluorescent-lit kitchen. Someone was playing

Aerosmith on a cheap little radio as they rolled out dough.
A cigarette dangled from their lip—the ashes flecked downward.

The bins were gray, wet at the bottom, pieces of white straw paper
stuck to their sides. "You can start off bussin tables," she said.
"Tuesday nights are usually slow, but Clayton called in sick
so there's a few booths that need cleanin. Can you do that?"
"Sure," I told her. "No problem."

                                                            "Good," she said.

I grabbed one of the bins from the stack and walked it over
to the empty booth closest to the door. Outside the window
it was black and starless, the Bud Light sign in the glass glowing
blue and red and white and humming softly, dead flies like spent
shotgun shells sprinkled beneath it on the wooden windowsill.

The tabletop was littered with plastic cups, the Coke left inside
made weak from melting ice, plates with chewed-up pizza crust
and smears of tomato sauce, balls of greasy napkins, dirty knives
and forks. I scraped it all up with my forearm and into the bin.

It made a loud noise and I turned around. Cindy was watching
me from the kitchen.

                                              So I reached down toward the vinyl seats,
which were cracked and leaking yellow foam stuffing, and picked up
a few napkins, then grabbed at something stuffed in the corner:
It was a long gray dirty sock, damp at the ends and torn. I looked at it.

Cindy had come up behind me now. "Ain't never seen that before,"
she was saying. "People are disgusting when they come in here to eat.
You think they do stuff like that in their own houses? Hell no."

I kept looking at the sock, felt humiliated by it somehow,
the fact that I would have to pick it up. "Well go on," she said.

"Can't leave it there." I wanted to put the bin down,
take off my cap, throw it on the ground, and walk out—
back into the long night that had deposited me into this dump:

The greasy walls, the dirty carpets, the gum stuck to the floor.
I looked at Cindy. She was still watching me. Waiting to see
what I was going to do. I set the bin on the tabletop. Pulled
a damp white rag from my back pocket.

                                                            Then I used it to pick
up the sock and drop it into the bin. "Hey, there you go," Cindy said.
"You popped your cherry." I looked away, my face warm.
"Wanna cigarette?" she said, winking and patting my shoulder.
"Now why don't you get the rest of these tables clean and I'll show
you how to work the cash register and make some pizzas."

She walked off. I didn't say anything. I just stood there for a second
before I finally picked up the bin and moved on to the next dirty table,
which seemed to be waiting for me in the gloom of this place
like someone hoping for a good sleep to get them out of the dark.

Truck

It was a tan Mazda B2200 that my dad bought
stripped down for under eight grand. He wrecked
it not long after he got it, but still drove
it anyway, getting pulled over more than once
and taken in for DWIs or otherwise
driving without a license.

And this is what he kept inside of it:
a sawed-off shotgun under the bench seat,
a pack of Marlboro reds, a Bowie knife
in the glove compartment, cans of Budweiser,
a box of Luden's wild cherry cough drops,
handkerchiefs, folded-up maps, Bic lighters,
pencils, tools, his suspended driver's license.

When he gave the truck to me years later,
the seats were torn and I had to cover them
with a quilt I found in one of our closets.
I put in a cheap radio and some speakers
in the back, the wires draped over the floor
like cobwebs.
                              The truck had over 300,000 miles
on it and by the time I got rid of it, I'd turned
over the odometer so that it showed all zeros.

Go-Kart

When we were in the third grade, I remember,
my parents bought my brother and me
a Go-Kart to ride around in the fields
behind our house.

It cost three-hundred-and-fifty dollars,
but we were so poor that we had to pay
on it in installments. Twenty-five bucks a month.

I remember, too, the man who would take
our checks: he had a handlebar mustache
which he kept waxed into two curled points
like the marks on the sides of those shoes
that all the other kids at school had
but which we couldn't afford, either.

(We got our shoes from Payless.)

Anyway:
It was a one-seater with a Briggs & Stratton
on the back, and we took turns going
back and forth—over and over—from our yard
to our grandma's, whose trailer was two doors down.

The times when my dad would run out of cigarettes
and had no way to get to the store, he'd take the Go-
Kart to my grandma's so he could bum some from her,
even though she smoked Carltons, and he had to tear
off the perforated filter just to get enough nicotine
to equal half of what he got from one of his Marlboros.

I remember all of these things—and this too:
how the only time I ever told my dad I loved him
his face turned red and he just looked
away from me and said, “I’m not going anywhere, babe.
What the hell are you telling me that for?”

And I remember that I never said that to him again.
Not even as he was dying ten years later
and I should have told him, but couldn’t bring
myself to make the words.

So today I remember this:
Just last week, I was racing my kids on Go-Karts
not much different from the one I used to have as a boy,
how the engines buzzed behind us as my wife watched,
took pictures with her phone. All of this
as we went around that slick oval track
over and over again, but always ending up
in the same place where we had started.

V.

Nostalgia

Going back to the place where I grew up,
fishing through a box of old photographs
to give to my mother on her birthday,
I find a picture of myself as a boy:
a Remington .410 Wingmaster in one hand,
three or four dead bobwhites in the other.

I put the picture in my back pocket,
decide to keep this one for myself—
I can't exactly tell you why—
and then I take my wife and kids outside
where we climb on one of the four wheelers
and ride down the horse trails in the woods.

We drive over steep clay banks and muddy swales
and into the shade of the pine thickets
which still surround the patch of land
where I was raised among what's wild,
my hair blowing back in the wind
as we pass horses, deer stands,
large brown rabbits, a hawk. And I show
my kids these things they never get to see.

We pass by my whole life, it seems,
spooling out before us like jute twine
never long enough to reach the end of the road
and then, before we know it, we're back
in the clearing where we started off.

They used to say nostalgia was a disease,
literally a sickness for the past or home,
but I like to think that instead of being sick

I simply long to be the boy I was
so as to better pass on this world
to my children. I'm telling you
I want my kids to carry this with them
in their own lives, down their own roads,
which even though they lead away from home,
they're always returning, always coming back.

Early Morning in the Marsh

After we toss the black plastic decoys,
we paddle out across the marsh,
the gray horizon giving way to orange
as the sun wheels up above the reeds.

Their stalks are black silhouettes
against the cold, early-morning sky
as a vee of ducks scatters in the distance.

The oars scrape the sides of the pirogue
as it sways toward the duck-blind
and noses up against a muddy finger of earth.

Then we climb out as the mud and water suck
at our waders. We haul our shotguns
into the blind and straighten out the reeds
which are laced through sheets of chicken-wire
and stapled onto a frame of damp two by fours.

You say this should be good enough for now.

Then I watch you take the wooden duck call
from the frayed lanyard around your neck
and blow into it. We both wait and watch
the mallards, blue-winged teal, widgeon,
wood ducks and canvasbacks skim by overhead.

You raise your .12 gauge to your shoulder
and pick off a duck with each of your three shots.
The smell of gunpowder climbs into my nose
as the dead birds pirouette from the sky.

I watch you eject the smoking plastic shells
into the tall grass beside our blind,
then look off into the distance and watch
the rest of the ducks fly away:
like a handful of tossed gravel—
a missed opportunity.

After Quail Hunting

In this picture, a .410's in my hand,
pointing skyward. I'm wearing
camouflage. I'm eight years old.
In my left hand, I'm holding
a couple of quail that we shot
in a field behind our single-wide—
the same trailer where I once locked
myself in one of the bedroom closets
and was too afraid to call out for help
so I just struggled with the door
until my uncle finally heard the noise.
He came in from where he was sitting
in the den watching the Saints game on TV
and pulled the door open to let me out.

I remember how incredibly sad he looked
that I hadn't asked for help or anything,
how instead I'd just kept pushing
on that cheap, brown wooden door
over and over and over as if it might
open on its own and let me go free.

And I can still remember those quail.
How we flushed them from the weeds
and how they rose up into the sky
like steam coming off a stack of dishes
sitting in the drainboard, freshly-washed
and waiting overnight in the dark
for someone to come along and put
them away where they belonged.

The Cast

When I was twelve I broke my wrist
and had to get a cast put over it until it healed.
That thing went all the way up to my shoulder,
making my whole arm the shape of a crooked L.

I couldn't eat, couldn't write, couldn't even bathe
without a significant amount of effort, so how on earth
was I supposed to shoot my .410, I wondered,
if I wanted to go duck hunting with my father?

My dad's solution was simple: he just cut the cast
halfway off, using a rusty hacksaw blade to slice
through the plaster, its dust like snow
piling up on the floor of the tool shed,
the cotton that was wrapped around my skin
torn apart like strands of matted horse hair.

*

When we went back to the doctor
so that I could have the cast properly removed,
the man was astounded—no, disgusted—
by what my father had done to me.
He told him as much. He said my arm
would never have a chance to heal correctly
thanks to my dad and his poor parenting.
What an injustice, the doctor said,
shaking his head and sucking at his teeth.

Then I listened to his tiny electric saw
as it went through the rest of the cast and pulled it

from my weak and skinny arm, its high-pitched buzz
whining as the sweaty plaster finally came free.

I could tell my father was embarrassed as we left,
but that doctor was wrong: my arm healed up just fine
and it had helped me kill a nice little passel of ducks that year,
despite the injustice he thought my dad had caused.

Blood River, Springfield, Louisiana

I'm hauling the boat I just bought last summer
behind my little pick-up truck down Highway 22,
my wife and kids are behind me in her van,
and I turn off onto a muddy gravel road
leading to a boat launch on the Tickfaw River.

Since my father never taught me how to drive a boat,
much less launch one into a body of water,
its dark embrace enveloping that smooth hull
as if it's falling into a pile of cool bedsheets,
I have to rely on what here in Louisiana
would be considered simple common sense,
though this is not so simple or common to me at all.

My foot quivers on the clutch as I back up
to where the gravel road ends at a concrete ramp
over which two people can back their trailers in at once
side-by-side, and then ease their boats into the river.
I pull the parking brake once my trailer's submerged,
get out my truck and walk knee-deep into the oily water.
Then I turn the winch until the boat is free
and I can pull it by its soaking hawser
to one of the pilings at the edge of the dock.

You see, I was born and raised here,
out in the country up around Folsom
if you want to get specific about it,
but I missed out on some of the best parts
since my dad was always too drunk
or too busy or just too damned angry
to show me how to do these things himself:
like boating, fishing, how to skin a deer.

I tie the boat off so I can park my truck
and meet my family in the weeded lot,
grab the life jackets, and help drag the ice chest,
which is packed with sandwiches my wife made,
some chips, and a tiny passel of Cokes and beers.

And here I am trying to make up for my past
by showing my kids these things
that I don't even really know myself,

and I wonder if my dad would be proud of me
for taking my family out on the water
like he always talked about doing, but never did.

We climb in the boat and head toward the Blood River,
the wind blowing my kids' hair back as we speed up
and the channel widens, spooling out before us
before it splits and curves into a nice shaded spot
where we drop the anchor and jump into the water:
the river's warm with patches of cold
that wrap around your legs and chest
and every now and then you can feel a fish glide by.

This is new to all of us, but I swear
it's as though we've done it a thousand times—
since I was a kid myself.

Photograph of My Father

You're standing in the kitchen of that old trailer
that you rented for us on Davidson Road
and where we lived for a couple of months
while you cleared some land just north of here in Folsom
to put another trailer that you were going to buy brand new.

I remember that one of the toilets in that old place
never flushed right and the whole trailer leaned
on its cinder blocks so that all the doors inside
hung wrong and they would creak open
in the middle of the night sometimes.

But there was a horse paddock in the front yard,
a couple of stalls where once I watched
you help deliver a colt and where another time
I saw you get kicked in the chest by its father.

There was also a great field where we rode Go-Karts
and where one time you pulled my brother and me
behind your truck on our scooters
with a piece of rope you found in the shed.

We hunted quail back there in that field too,
pitched baseballs, shot bows and arrows
at little paper targets. And we went fishing
in a pond that was on another man's land.

That's where you caught the fish you're holding
in this picture. It's a bass that for some reason
you called "Walter." Its silver scales and wide mouth
are open around your closed hand and its caudal fin
comes all the way down to your belt—
I swear that fish must've been three feet long.

You're smiling about as much as you ever did here:
your teeth aren't showing. Just a tight, hard grin
that's barely visible beneath your beard
and your beer-reddened face and cheeks.

You're also younger in this picture
than I am now, probably by at least five years,
and have only a dozen more left to live.
But of course you don't know that here.
How could you?

Behind you the counter's covered with grocery bags,
a box of Frosted Flakes, some pots and pans
and their lids. There's a sugar bowl, paper towels
a couple of two liter bottles of Coke, a coffee maker.

You're standing in front of that counter
and just to the right of a dingy yellow refrigerator—
you're wearing dark jeans and green hospital scrubs
that you got when you went to the Emergency Room
after you nailed your hand to a rabbit cage that time.
Do you remember that?

Anyway, this fish you're holding is staring out
past your thick, dark arms, past the mess
of our kitchen and the mess of the life you built
for us, but that was still somehow pretty good.

The Deep Woods

—after the opening line from Cormac McCarthy's Blood Meridian

See the boy. He is alone in a dark clearing.
He's surrounded by gray pines, webbed
together with deadfall and thick smoke
which is coming off his dying fire
like heavy fog over a morning lake.
The fire's black remnants lie smoldering
on a hard patch of earth before him.

The ground is damp at the boy's feet
and he sips from a dented canteen
the last of his water
tinged the color of cardboard
from the tannins in the ditch
where he had sloshed it up
just before he stopped here to rest.

And now he sits beside the trail. It twists
through the woods like a snake's intestines
and leads to where he'd been told
his father lives in a rundown shack.
This is where he plans to meet this man
though he never claimed the boy as his.
But he has made a promise, in theory,
that the boy thinks the man should keep.

He's been out here for days, this boy,
braving the cold, the rain, the darkness
all bearing down on him at once,
the only warmth the thought
of sharing a good meal with his father:

venison, maybe sweet potatoes
burnt black around the edges
over a scullery fire, its flame
as orange as the soft meat
that oozes out the skin like molten slag.

Now see the boy get up,
start once again for the crooked path
which will take him to where he wants to go.
But first watch him stop to let a deer leap
from out of a copse and then disappear,
its black eye a marble
shot into a sun-bleached two by four
reflecting nothing behind it
and looking only at what's ahead.

Refraction

A cold front blew through last night,
bringing with it gusting swales
of wind and rain,
which must've knocked the power out
while we were still asleep in bed.

The blinking red numbers
on the digital clock said 3AM,
though I don't think that was right.
Yet I got up from bed and stumbled
into the dark kitchen for a glass of water.

Then I cut the alarm, let the dog out,
and even though it's over a mile
away from here, I could hear a train
howling and screeching across the tracks
all the way from my front door.

It must have been the colder, thinner air
that helped the sound to make its way this far.
Refraction, I think it's called.
It was the only thing I could think of
as I stared at the spackling of stars overhead.

I imagined those damp gray cars,
could almost see them tattooed
with their bright graffiti, barreling past,
and that long, long trail of freighters and tanks,
all of it sliding quickly through the dark.

Then I heard the train's loud horn bellowing,
the metal on metal as it skirled

over the tracks. And I'm imagining this, too:
the wheels shooting up blue-white sparks
as the train heads north, past where I live
and into the long flat delta of Mississippi.

VI.

The King on Beale Street

The Mississippi curving brown and slow in the distance,
a soft alluvium spreading out beneath all that concrete
like a bowl of those hot grits they serve at The Arcade,
where he ate with Junior and Gene Smith, Red West
and Cliff Gleaves, all crammed up in an upholstered booth;

like the men waiting for a chair at Jim's Barber Shop,
where he got his hair cut and styled, a good clean shave.
Everyone knows his look—slicked back and coal black:

                                        a river that can swallow
up the whole town with one hard rain, and folks here
seem to know it too. It's in the way they move, man,
especially him, like he's walking on water—the only way
to get around in the Delta, where the ground's flat as a sponge
made out of mud.

Still you can just imagine him gliding down Beale Street,
young and dreaming and maybe even knowing already
who he was, that he was something special, but he stayed
humble just in case:
                                ushered moviegoers to their seats
at Loew's, worked at M. B. Parker's machine shop,
drove a delivery truck for Crown Electric. He ran
a drill press for a short spell at Precision Tool,
even lied about his age on an application once
to get a job.

                        And then he would stand looking
through the tall, stocked windows of Lansky Bros.,
dreaming about one day maybe owning the whole place
or at least some of those fine, fine clothes they had in there.

But he didn't make much money. No, not yet.
He was still poor, after all. Delta poor, the kind of poor
that could change how a person thought about the world
and what their place was in it.

And so he lived with his parents at Lauderdale Courts,
the low income housing project where he played guitar
in the community laundry room, the glimmer of his future
closing in on him like the Mississippi, steadily testing
its banks, that great flood all but inevitable now,
so much water stretching itself out over those flat fields
of cotton like the light from the sun slowly filling the sky.

How many people would have said it was impossible
for a boy from Tupelo, someone like him,
to come to Memphis, then get known all over the world
like he did? Maybe they'd say it started when he played
that gig in Clarksdale in 1955, just days after he turned
twenty. Maybe they'd say he stopped at those crossroads,
the ones Robert Johnson sang about—with bluesmen selling
their souls to the devil. That's probably what they'd think
he did to get all that money. All those songs and movies
and fancy cars. But they'd be wrong. Folks who'd believe
something like that about a man don't understand anything
about having vision, of having a faith in yourself so deep
you can feel it in your bones.

After all, he was just a boy
whose daddy served eight months out at Parchman Farm
for altering a four-dollar check—about the same amount
he'd later pay Sam Phillips to cut that double-sided acetate
for his mama: then spreading that sweet, sweet gospel
of music out all over the Delta, a swath of land growing
so large that nobody but him could have ever imagined it.

Graceland

To get there they bus you in from a lot across the street
brimming with tourists from all over the world.
People who came here to Memphis, Tennessee, just for him.
And you wonder if they think this is really America:
all the diners, museums, the Heartbreak Hotel.
A gaudy pink Cadillac, and even an airplane
glistened with rain.
                                        The kitsch of rock n roll.

But when you finally pull in, the house is smaller
than what you'd think. And, walking through it,
you get the feeling that the man who lived here
would've given just about anything to be normal.
To be like everyone else. To be here even now.
Walking among all these anonymous faces
and crowding the tiny rooms where he once lived—
just hoping for a glimpse of something magic
so that you might turn into someone else,
anyone that's not yourself.

Blume with Chicken

January 1986, Lowndes County, Mississippi
—after a photograph by Birney Imes

It's been a long night. The morning comes up slow and gray.
And cold. You can almost hear all the rust settle and crack
on the old appliances lined up against the cinderblock walls,
the grease-darkened windows settling in their frames.

And Old Man Blume Triplett standing out there in the gravel lot
of what was once his daddy's store—Whispering Pines, he called it.

He's got a cigar in his mouth, the stub left over from after breakfast.
Same thing he has every day: two runny eggs, two pieces of burnt toast,
and four strips of bacon shimmering in their own hot grease. His doctor
said all of this will kill him one day, but Blume just said, "What won't?"

The flannel jacket he's wearing does just enough to keep off the cold,
but does well too to cover those faded blue tattoos on his forearms—
the ones he got in Hawaii when he was in the navy, the only time he ever left
Mississippi. The only time he ever plans to. You fight for your country
when it calls on you, his daddy had told him. And so he did.

And now he takes care of the old store, even though it's closed down
and dead, waiting for the ground to take it back to dirt and loam and rock.
But he still keeps it up while he can. He just spraypainted one of the letters
in the sign yesterday, as a matter of fact—the white outline of the "G"

still
stenciled over the gravel like one of his old tattoos.

Blume stands there

holding
a hen in his arms, stroking the soft golden-brown feathers of her neck
as she takes
in the warmth of him. Just like a child would. But Blume never had
any children.
It's just him and the bird and this run-down store his daddy left him
when he passed.
And it's a cold, cold day for Mississippi, and they'll both take all the
heat they can get.

Man with Mouthless Fish

Phillip, Mississippi, 1982

—after a photograph by Birney Imes

That old clock on the wall in her daddy's store has been stuck
on the same time for ten years. 3:04, it says.
And people can't remember anymore if it stopped
in the morning or in the afternoon.

Carl likes to tell the little girl
that they stopped it on the day she was born. To mark the occasion.
She's always liked that little story. She's always liked Carl, too.

In fact, she calls him Uncle Carl, and she lets him help her bait her lines
when they all go fishing on the mornings when she doesn't have school.

After they get back, her daddy lets her pick whatever she wants
off the shelf: Snickers, Now & Later, Butterfingers, a bottle of RC Cola.
But first, as dawn fingers the black line of pine trees hugging the shoals,
they'll fish, casting their lines and nets into the Little Tallahatchie,

the river stretching wide and dark in places, logs easing over its surface:
a thick brown milk teeming with catfish and other things unseen, floating
all the way down from God-knows-where.

The little girl thinks on those things as she stands behind the cooler in her daddy's store,
watching him and Uncle Carl as they show off the fish they caught

today.

Her daddy had scooped it up with a net, and they had all marveled
at its deformities: no mouth, a cataracted eye, no fins to speak of.
How did it survive this long, the little girl wonders:

all that dark, dark water above it, pushing down on it as it inched its
way
through riversilt and the myriad ribs of sand as that thick brown
string of water
turned and curved and fanned itself out into its own wild version of an
open gaping mouth?

Stoop

Hermanville, Mississippi, 1981
—after a photograph by Birney Imes

The concrete stoop is cracked, a fissure like a broken bone
running right across its lower half: a toothless, crooked smile.
Its surface is spackled with damp cigarette butts, a can of Bud
resting between a set of workboots, greasy and dust-skeined.

A group of men sits there—behind them a spine of stairs,
some of the wooden slats missing, others warped and aged
but all of them leading up into darkness, to some hovel maybe,
where most of these men go to sleep off their day's labors,
only to wake up tomorrow and do it all over again.

One man is tossing a boiled peanut into his mouth. Another one
screws the cap onto a plastic bottle of Coke. They're talking.
Trying to push the worries of the day beneath the surface,
like the alluvium that shifts and flows under all of that concrete
and how it could just disappear with one really good spell of rain.

Yet there's one man whose eyes you can't quite see. He's wearing
a denim shirt, jeans spattered with grease and paint. A nub
of cigarette juts out from his fingers. And he's completely still—
so still that you can make out the words on his hat. It's an old
trucker's hat,
askew on his head, and it says, in white letters, "Here I Am."

Turk's Place

Leflore County, Mississippi, 1989
—after a photograph by Birney Imes

A strand of Christmas lights is stretched
across the clapboard wall in front—
even though it's not Christmas, and won't be
for a long time coming. They look good
from the road though, if you can even call
this a road. It's really just a scrim of gravel
on a dirt lane full of wheelruts and a puddle
where you'll bottom out if you don't slow down.
I don't care how bad you want to get there.
Or leave. But wait. Don't go just yet.
Not without noticing all these trees first.
How they seem like giant paintbrushes
that God Himself might've used to slather
on all that dark blue paint in the sky.
You might as well look. The sun's been gone
for a while now and there's not much else
to do here anyway. That I can promise you.

Magic City

Falcon, Mississippi, 1989

—after a photograph by Birney Imes

See the building. If you can still even call it that:
In the two holes out front where windows once were
are six black slats of wood, the words "Magic City"
stenciled in red, and on one of them there's a sticker
that says "I Love Music." The door is painted
red too and has a bright gold star in the middle,
just above an old mail slot that's covered now
with a piece of white paper to keep people
from shoving stuff through it.

There's a couple
of metal latches on the outside of that old door
where padlocks went through when it was closed,
but someone's standing there now, holding it
partway open. You can see them looking out.

There are two by fours holding up the roof,
which is covered with tar paper and gravel.
But the men under it don't seem to notice—
or care—as they lean against that fresh wood,
smiling and smoking, probably imagining
what the camera's lens might capture of them.
If it's going to catch their good sides.

The Pink Pony Cafe

Darling, Mississippi, 1985
—after a photograph by Birney Imes

A young girl. Framed inside of a wooden doorway.
But there's no door. And nothing but darkness behind her.
She's wearing a pink shirt, a red jacket, a red belt. Jeans.

Looking out from the threshold of a building that's made
of broken red bricks, rusted sheet metal, a stained screen
covering this place's one filthy window. Which itself looks
down and onto a muddy yard littered with cans,
brown bottles, and crumpled batons of aluminum foil:
leftovers from last night's supper.

There's an upended chair on the roof. And you wonder:
Did the same wind that bent all the tin eaves upward like that—
covering the sign that says "Pink Pony Cafe"
so that you can hardly make out the gray letters anymore—
toss that chair up there? You could ask the girl

who's standing in the doorway, but she's distracted.
Her family's already started dinner, their long shadows
cast across the brick and wood like the last remnants
of an atomic blast, that bright flash leaving
nothing behind but an image on a wall:

a bench, a mother, a father. Their children.

The Evangelist

—for Elvis Presley, performing "Unchained Melody" (1977)
two months before his death

When he was a boy in Tupelo he'd go outside
if the moon was full—just a lonely white disc
in the sky—and he'd sing to his twin brother
who had died at birth. His mama told him to do that,
and so he did.

And he kept trying, his whole life, to do all the right things,
to make everybody happy—even God—
and maybe he did that too.

Because it's hard not to imagine that God doesn't weep
every time you hear him sing, even though he's out of breath
and gleaming sweat, and someone has to hold his microphone
for him. There's just something holy in his voice.

It's the only way to say it.

Or it's something lonely.
A river widening and widening until it becomes the sea.
Or maybe it's something sweet: something that says
to wait for him, because he's finally coming home.

About the Author

DAVID ARMAND was born and raised in Louisiana. He has worked as a drywall hanger, a draftsman, and as a press operator in a flag printing factory. From 2017-2019, he served as Writer-in-Residence at Southeastern Louisiana University, where he is currently assistant professor of creative writing. In 2010, he won the George Garrett Fiction Prize for his first novel, *The Pugilist's Wife*, which was published by Texas Review Press. He has since published three more novels, two collections of poetry, and a memoir. His latest book, *Mirrors*, is forthcoming from the University of Louisiana at Lafayette Press.